THE
WELCOMING
HOUSE

THE WELCOMING HOUSE

Jane Schwab
and Cindy Smith

WRITTEN WITH JUDITH NASITIR
FOREWORD BY BUNNY WILLIAMS

RIZZOLI
NEW YORK

New York · Paris · London · Milan

For our parents, who taught us about sincere and generous hospitality by living and entertaining graciously— and always welcoming one more to any gathering of family and friends—and for our husbands and families, who inspire us to do the same.

TABLE OF CONTENTS

FOREWORD

A number of years ago, when working on a project in Charlotte, North Carolina, I was taken to a shop called Circa. It had never happened to me before, but when I entered the shop and looked around, I realized I wanted everything in there. I was then taken on a tour of the design part of the shop, where there were samples of every beautiful fabric folded neatly on the shelves. Who were these designers? Well, they were Jane Schwab and Cindy Smith, two amazingly talented ladies and the nicest, kindest, most stylish people I have ever met. They have become dear friends.

Now they have created this gorgeous book, which not only opens the doors to many stunning interiors but also helps explain in exquisite detail their design philosophy. They take you through their thought process on room functions and planning. Their use of color, their selections of elegant furniture, their choice of accessories, and their attention to detail is all shared on every page.

Both Jane and Cindy grew up with what they call the open-door policy, and they still continue to carry it out in their own homes. In this book, they share with the reader their tips for making a home feel welcoming and for entertaining with style, but ease. I have been lucky enough to be a guest of honor at a dinner that was held outside on the terrace, with dinner served at one very long table, so beautifully set with purple hurricanes and simple flowers. Delicious food, candlelight, and fun guests all made it a night to remember. Both hostesses were so relaxed that you never would have guessed what effort they had put into that magical dinner.

This will be a book to treasure, to make notes from, and to be inspired by. And I am sure the next time I am shopping at the markets in France or anywhere there is a great antiques market, I will happily run into Jane and Cindy and hope I can find the treasures first. If not, however, I know I can always buy it from them, and we shall all laugh and talk about how much we love what we do.

—*Bunny Williams*

INTRODUCTION

A house with an open door is like a friend with an open heart: inviting, generous of spirit, and constant to the core. It's a place where welcome crosses the threshold and is palpable from the curb. Both of us grew up in houses with open doors. We cherish that quality in our own homes, and we work very hard to instill it in the homes that we design for others. Although we have different yet complementary personal styles of decoration, we share a similar, deeply rooted sense of what a home should be. Home is shelter, of course. But it's far, far more than just the roof and walls that keep us warm, safe, and comfortable, as essential as those are. The indoor and outdoor rooms where we gather for a casual meal, an elegant dinner, a festive fundraiser, or a holiday celebration are the places where we can give the best of ourselves to our families and our friends. At Circa, we feel that all the rooms we design should meet everyday needs beautifully and also adapt gracefully to extraordinary ones. The best rooms, the most wonderful houses, should wrap all those who enter in a warm embrace whether they're there for an evening, a weekend, or even an extended visit. We believe the essence of hospitality begins at home.

Mastering the art of the inviting house involves a thoughtful combination of architecture and interior design. Much of a home's quality of graciousness comes from the way its spaces flow, inside and out. Considerations include the proportions of the individual rooms, the ways we get from one room to another, the manner in which the light of day travels through the interiors, the pathways to the outdoors, and the style of the gardens that surround it.

A proper sense of entry is important, as is a natural separation between shared spaces such as living rooms, kitchens, and dining rooms and private ones, like bedrooms and baths. Choreographing easy, pleasant transitions from one room to the next and from indoors to outdoors helps not only you

We believe that for interiors to be successful aesthetically and comfortably, they need the combination of familiarity and originality, lightness and depth, and just a few little sly twists.

but also your guests to relax. Designating certain areas for specific uses at different times of the day—such as a screened porch for coffee and a newspaper in the morning and a glass of wine at the end of the day—is a lovely option. Creating multifunctional, adaptable gathering places in and out of doors to welcome and entertain one person as comfortably as many—that's what we feel design is all about.

Well-appointed rooms can help start you off on the right foot every morning. The happiest mix of textures and colors, fabrics and furnishings, lighting and accessories pleases the senses, which is important. Lovely surroundings help make everyday chores a pleasure. While our natural first responses to a room's colors, patterns, textures, finishes, and light are sensory ones, the graciousness we feel in a particular environment also depends on how well the elements of that environment address matters of practicality and function. Beautiful tables are divine, but even more so when they're proportioned and positioned so that you can put a lamp on them or set down a drink. The most comfortable sofas and chairs are imperative, but so is arranging them into inviting groups to encourage conversation. Sufficient wall space in the dining room—and easy access to the kitchen—is what allows you to prepare a proper buffet and present serving items in a convenient and elegant way. There's necessity, too, especially in the little things—like stashing a basket for towels by the back door so that when your dog comes in, you can wipe him off, or keeping a blanket on the sofa to hide the dog hair if that same dog lords over you, your family, and the living room.

Part of design is seeing things that you like or love and imagining the ways you can modify or change them to suit your needs and environment. Something has to trigger the creative urge, and inspiration can come from anywhere. Whenever we travel, whether it's with our families or on buying trips for Circa, we always see things that we want to translate to Charlotte, North Carolina, our home. We both love Europe—France especially. When we're at the flea market in Paris, in the French countryside, or visiting the homes of friends, we always revel in—and note for future reference—the unique qualities of presentation and the details large and small. We'll take delight in—and a mental note of—a tabletop arrangement, unforced but so distinctive, with exceptional flowers, linens, stemware, and dinnerware. It's that seemingly effortless touch that inspires us and provides a catalyst for rethinking and reinterpreting what's natural, beautiful, romantic, and easy, yet also individual and imaginative.

We believe that rooms should be timeless, yet of their time. For us, that means taking a traditional, more European approach to decorating, which mixes the old and the "now" in balanced and harmonious interiors. We love the patina of age and the expressivity that beautiful antiques can add to every room. But homes should have a vacation spirit too—in other words, they should be relaxing but also a bit exciting. Achieving that effect is as much a matter of practicality and efficiency as it is of aesthetics.

One of our goals is to have the rooms and houses we design last for many years. Because our underlying desire is to provide each client with surroundings that have staying power, we tend to prefer neutral backgrounds. Our style includes a carefully calibrated mix of casual, comfortable upholstery with more decorative pieces, such as an interesting chair or two, so that our clients can dress a room up or down as they wish. We tend to use natural materials, clean lines, and subtle color and pattern on upholstery, walls, and curtains (often straightforward panels in rich fabrics) because we find them to be both stylish and unpretentious. When we need to add pizzazz, we use a careful selection of accessories—everything from amethyst glass to pillows with dressmaker details to fine art—which provide necessary jolts of color, pattern, and personality. If we feel a small room needs waking up, we might hang an oversize chandelier. If we have the opportunity, we'll create a breakfast nook with a banquette around an oversize table so that the family can gather comfortably in the morning and use it to entertain friends throughout the day and evening. If we're working on a dining porch, a loggia, or an outdoor spot for entertaining, we like to incorporate the view of the garden or the landscape.

For us, the overall plan always comes first, the big picture before the details. Mapping the ideal of what a room or a house wants to look like—to be—points us toward our ultimate destination, design-wise. Should we not be able to get there all at once, the plan helps us prioritize which gradual steps to take toward our goal, and in what order. We often tell our clients to start with the family room and to make it as comfortable as possible, because that's where the family and guests gather. The master bedroom is another priority for us, because it is the space where each of us goes to recharge ourselves nightly. In fact, we believe the private areas of the house—the master bedroom and bath—are the rooms where we should treat ourselves as we would our most welcome and cared-for guests. When bedrooms and baths are soothing and equipped for every need, they act as an elixir and help us face each day fully fortified.

When friends and family come to stay, we like for them to feel at home and truly welcome. We want to provide them with whatever they might need in their bedroom: a space to put a suitcase, a place to hang clothes, an empty chest for unpacking if the guest is staying for several days, a TV, a comfortable chair, and a bench on which to prop their feet. Plus, there are all the little but important necessities that help make a guest feel well cared for: tissues, notepads, shampoo, magazines, phone chargers, bottled water, and so on. And then there are the extras that we all love for the thoughtfulness they represent, such as a bit of chocolate, a bottle of prosecco, or after-dinner liqueur.

We are great believers in the power of presentation, especially when we entertain. A few special moments and a surprise here and there help to make a party memorable. Good food is always key, but so are finishing touches like the table setting, bar arrangement, and cocktail area. Most important of all is making your guests feel cared for and content. That means not only must you anticipate in advance any needs that might arise during the party, but that you should also enjoy the party yourself. When you do, people leave with a great feeling . . . and that's what they hold dear.

As designers, we have the opportunity to witness how our clients' houses work on a day-to-day basis and, on occasion, for a party. We both love to entertain, and we have so many wonderful resources at our fingertips that, when they ask, it's a pleasure to help our clients prepare for their special occasions. Whether it's dinner for twelve or a garden party for one hundred, we're happy to discuss ideas and specific solutions. Helping them let their houses shine is the icing on the cake after all our hard work on the interior and exterior rooms. It's a wonderful privilege to see how a house is used and an honor to experience the joy that clients get from having their homes be what they want them to be.

Our clients often tell us how much they love walking through the doors of their homes. Every time they cross their threshold, they say they feel as if they've entered a special place, one that's restful, replenishing, and exciting. Part of getting a house to feel that way involves editing. Our philosophy is that if something isn't functional, beautiful, or possessed of sentimental value, it should go. When there is too much clutter, there's havoc: the eye is constantly busy, so it's impossible to relax. We help people clear away that clutter yet still reveal their personalities in their homes. We listen closely to how they want to live, how their rooms need to function on a day-to-day basis, where they sit, where they watch TV—all of that. We want them to express themselves through their choices in furnishings and fabrics, in the way they plan their gardens, and through their collections of objects and heirlooms.

We have always found that in design and entertaining, the key to spontaneity is preparation. When you have the essentials, planning is a breeze and improvising becomes easy and fun. No matter the scale, entertaining at home should never be overwhelming. Both of us have made a concerted effort to have supplies on hand so that we're ready for any occasion. We try to help prepare our clients to do the same. When they have what they need within easy reach, they'll never feel as if it's just too much work to entertain.

Entertaining is an opportunity to share the best of yourself with others, after all. A gracious home is the same. That's why we think both are so important and why we prepare so carefully to the last detail. When a party succeeds, when a home is wonderfully welcoming, it creates a mood and an emotion that lasts. Memories are life's great gift to us all. They only happen if—and when—you open the door.

RESPECTING TRADITION

SOME HOUSES LOOK SO FRIENDLY AND INVITING from the street that they make us smile every time we drive by them. Our lime-washed-brick colonial has always had that effect on me. Martin Evans Boyer (1893–1970), architect of some of Charlotte's loveliest residences, designed and built the house for a client in 1923. When my husband and I purchased it in 1999, it was already beautifully planted with boxwood, *Camellia sasanqua*, and other indigenous species.

We engaged McAlpine Tankersley Architecture of Montgomery, Alabama, to help us modernize and renovate the house for our family's lifestyle while remaining true to its original form. We added a family room on one end, a master suite on the other, a garden room, a guesthouse, and a loggia. We also opened up the kitchen and extended the screened porch. Ben Page, our landscape architect, designed the pool area, repositioned the driveway, added a pea-gravel motor court, and selected plantings to suit the house's history. The progression feels so natural that you'd never know what's original and what's new.

With shades of Georgian- and Adam-style symmetry, the Schwabs' cottage
Colonial has an approachable, friendly scale.

In design and decoration, pretty is wonderful, but it's far from everything. Practicality and function always come first, because if a room doesn't work, who will use it?

The original house had great bones. The renovation has strengthened them, establishing an easy, graceful flow and seamless transitions. It has also made entertaining, which we love to do, a pleasure and a breeze; conveniently positioned storage places for refreshments, linens, cutlery, and glasses ensure we're always set to go.

Now a true gathering place, the kitchen opens naturally to the family, garden, and dining rooms and the loggia. Elegant and intimate, the dining room can seat twenty-four at two round tables. The living room offers two seating areas, a fireplace, and windows on three sides. The family room is an everyday spot for us and Margo and Marshall, our beagles who definitely rule the roost.

In addition to our ground-floor master suite, we have upstairs bedrooms and the guesthouse. With grown children and growing families, it's nice for each to have their own space when visiting.

One of the joys of living in this house comes from the richness of its architectural detail. For that, we are thankful. A previous owner went to great lengths to preserve some of this region's vanishing architectural history. In 1958, she salvaged all the moldings from an eighteenth-century house in Annapolis, Maryland, as it was being demolished and installed them in the living room and dining room here. Those 1780s pilasters, crowns, doors, and over doors add such loveliness to these rooms and such history too.

In the foyer, an eighteenth-century French painted demilune console reflects the curve of the archway. Flanking a silver tray are etched-crystal lamps.

For us, architecture and decoration go hand in hand. It's wonderful when each is good on its own. When the two combine to create a truly harmonious environment, even the most mundane chores can become a pleasure.

With windows on three sides, the living room has wonderful light. The sofa sits along the one uninterrupted wall. Between the windows, we've placed an eighteenth-century walnut secretary and a French barometer. The antique Oushak creates a landscape for two inviting seating groups. The eighteenth-century mantel is among the architectural elements salvaged from a house in Annapolis. At night, lit candles in the hurricanes give life to the room's far side.

*Subtlety is very important to us. So is variety.
Both can provide the wry twist that will help
make a room and a home interesting, pleasing,
and personal—timeless too.*

SETTING A BEAUTIFUL TABLE

NEVER UNDERESTIMATE THE POWER OF PRESENTATION. A festive, fun table helps make an occasion out of a meal, however simple or grand. There's no great secret to setting a lovely table. We always start by choosing a color. You might opt for one of the hues in your china pattern, particularly if that pattern contains fruit or flowers. You could also develop a palette from something wonderful blooming in your garden, especially if the flower petals pick up a tone in the color of your walls or chair fabric. Once you have a color theme, you can build your table decor around it. You could put the blossoms in silver goblets, if you have them, or in something else pretty at hand. The same goes for the crystal or the stemware; if it happens to be colored and in the same family of hues that you've already selected, that's even better.

IF YOU'RE SETTING A TABLE FOR A BUFFET instead of a seated dinner, you might consider making a statement with your flowers. You could arrange them in a crystal ice bucket and use that as the centerpiece. You can array all the necessary dining accoutrements on one side or the other: flatware and napkins, stemware and dinnerware, and, of course, the food, beautifully laid out on appropriate serving pieces.

ADD CANDLELIGHT HIGH AND LOW to create instant atmosphere and another memory to share with friends and family.

WE BELIEVE YOU SHOULD USE WHAT YOU HAVE rather than letting your possessions linger in a cabinet or a drawer unloved. Your silver flatware, for instance, isn't just for dressy occasions. And your mother's and your grandmother's beautiful old silver serving pieces and coffee service can certainly add a quiet gleam to the dull glow of polished mahogany, oak, cherry, and walnut. If you want to use those pieces but you're concerned that they may be too showy or off-putting, try pairing them with straw placemats or earthenware plates to make them feel less dressy and more up-to-the-moment.

THE ARCHITECTURE OF A ROOM may dictate much of what happens within its four walls, but architecture doesn't determine your every last choice. The design details are up to you. If your dining room has an inherent formality, you can play that up or tone it down with your furniture, linens, tableware, lighting, and flowers. You can set a very pretty table for everyday use. And on special occasions, you can lay a more formal table than usual. Whatever the situation, make the most of it. One of life's more reliable pleasures is sharing a meal with family and friends. Setting a lovely table helps ensure that each meal is memorable.

Straw placemats add a rustic touch to the refinement of the silver,
china, and crystal that make the table so pretty. Layers of yellow and yellow-orange
create a unifying theme for a table setting with great variety.

The kitchen is the heart of the house. With the family room off one side and the garden room off the other, it's also part of the traffic pattern. When a room doubles as a hallway, as our garden room (opposite) also does, it's even more important to include the things that you love.

A family room is the epitome of a multifunctional room. Whether it's a gathering spot for the entire family to read or watch TV or the go-to setting for an impromptu dinner by the fire on a winter evening or a late afternoon cup of tea, it's a room where casual comfort reigns.

Like the kitchen, the family room has a white-painted beadboard ceiling. The panels over the fireplace conceal a flat-screen TV. Extra-comfy seating, covered in dog-friendly neutral linens, encourages lounging and reading.

An eighteenth-century French settee sits under a Jared Sanders landscape of
Wyoming cottonwood trees at the end of the main ground-floor hallway. The master bedroom
(opposite) is serene in soft shades of green, blue, and cream.

Soft greens and soft blues are calming in spirit and restful on the eyes— wonderful colors for the room where we begin and end each day.

Punches of blue in the glass lamp, the pillows, and the blue-painted tole sconces accent the palette of gentle greens. At the foot of the bed, an antique Oushak rests atop the silk and linen carpet. At the window, panels of charcoal-and-green-striped silk drop from silver-leafed rods with gold accents.

In our octagonal master bath, twin vanities flank a freestanding tub. A bronze and crystal chandelier hangs overhead. Wood venetian blinds and lined wool sheers cover the windows. A wood-plank floor is soft, comfortable, and durable.

Hospitality really does begin at home. There are many thoughtful ways to make sure your guests feel the warmth of your welcome and the pleasure that you take in their company.

Our guesthouse includes a pair of painted faux-bamboo double beds, each with an upholstered ottoman at its foot. We've used natural sisal on the floor. The eighteenth-century French armoire houses the TV and extra storage. A chair in the bathroom comes in handy for extra towels or as a place to lay a bathrobe.

In the guesthouse bedroom, an arrangement of garden flowers in
a silver cup is a thoughtful note. An antique Swedish desk contains all the
necessaries for note writing and a place to charge electronics.

We're particular about what items we think
a guest bedroom or guesthouse ought to include.
The golden rule of hospitality, however,
always remains the same: comfort comes first
and preparation is essential.

GUEST ROOM ESSENTIALS

WHEN WE HAVE FAMILY AND FRIENDS TO STAY, we always want to provide them with as many comforts of home as we possibly can—and more. If you have space for a guesthouse, you'll have the best of all possible worlds in terms of both shared experiences and private time. If you don't, a well-appointed guest room will certainly help make a visit memorable.

WHEN SPACE PERMITS, YOU MIGHT CONSIDER FURNISHING the guest room or guesthouse with a pair of double beds so that it can accommodate both young families and couples. If there's space to stow a suitcase and a closet for hanging up clothes, so much the better. If your guests plan to visit for several days, they might wish to put away their things in a chest of drawers or an armoire—much neater and nicer than living out of a suitcase. A comfortable chair for reading or watching TV is a pleasure, and so is a pull-up bench or an ottoman for propping up feet.

IF YOUR GUESTHOUSE HAS ROOM for a separate bar area, consider stocking the refrigerator with fruit, yogurt, bottled water, juice, beer, and/or wine. A coffeemaker and a microwave, plus glasses, mugs, and utensils, allow guests who are early risers to be self-sufficient.

WHENEVER WE HAVE THE OPPORTUNITY to work with an architect on guest rooms, we try to ensure that the rooms include closets large enough so that guests can unpack their suitcase in the closet and operate from there. We also try to make sure the closet includes a shelf where guests can plug in a phone, an iPad, and any other electronic devices, so that the bedroom itself is just for relaxing. Everything stays neater that way.

AS FOR THE SMALLER NECESSITIES, our list probably looks a lot like yours: tissues, notepads, a telephone, shampoo, lotion, crisp sheets, extra plush towels, a reading lamp, toiletries, and, most of all, the pleasure of your company.

When we extended the porch off the living room, we added the columns and replaced the glass with screens. A fan overhead moves the air on warm days. We like to paint the ceilings of porches and loggias pale blue or green; here, I've used Farrow & Ball's Light Blue.

The loggia between the main house and the guesthouse is a lovely spot for dining alfresco, even when it rains. It's just off the kitchen, so easy and accessible. A potted plant is a constant centerpiece; here, it's lamb's ear.

Life in this house moves effortlessly between indoors and outdoors. The French doors in the garden room open onto the pool area, which is paved in Pennsylvania bluestone. The chaises and tables are teak; the cushions are covered in a Sunbrella fabric. For an outdoor celebratory dinner (following spread), we opted for a palette of amethyst, lavender, and gray.

44

For a large seated dinner, you may opt to set several small tables or one large one. Each offers design advantages. One long surface creates a wonderful stage for a large-scale tableau; several smaller ones enhance an intimate effect.

SPECIAL OCCASION TABLES

THERE'S A DEFINITE LOGIC TO DESIGN, no matter the scale. Whether you're creating a room intended to endure or an event for one night only, all the same elements come into play. We always consider context, purpose, and scale, function and ornament, color and pattern, matte and sheen, and atmosphere and mood. And because design is something of a domino effect, we also consider how each choice affects all the others.

IF YOU'RE HOSTING A LARGE SEATED DINNER for a special occasion, for instance, you must first decide where your stage is—that is, indoors or outdoors—and what the proportions and conditions of that area permit. Will you set one long table? Or would several smaller ones be preferable? Both are lovely options. Each has distinct advantages that may suit one type of occasion better than another, but both create the intimacy at the table that serves to enhance the mood. Ultimately, it's a matter of personal choice.

TO CELEBRATE A DEAR, RENOWNED FRIEND in from out of town, we opted to set one long table (see previous spread) on the poolside terrace outside the garden room. A long table offers a wonderful opportunity to create a vivid, dramatic effect from the repetition of elements that are inherent to the art of setting a beautiful table.

ONCE WE'VE DECIDED ON THE SEATING PLAN, we tend to select a color palette that will suit the season and the china pattern. Purples and grays are the palette here; the purples provide a pop of color that contrasts wonderfully with the surrounding greenery and the soft gray of the linen tablecloths (shades of the Pennsylvania bluestone pavers). Five lavender and gray runners with a hint of gold section the length of the table into more intimate areas, as do the five amethyst hurricanes running down the center of the table. Amethyst water glasses bring the color closer to the table's edge. Low arrangements of purple flowers with greenery—sweet peas, lamb's ear, boxwood, hydrangea, and allium—in baskets bring the garden to the tabletop and a touch of rusticity to the refinement. A pair of eighteenth-century French faux-bois candelabra adds symmetry and height to the presentation.

FOR BOTH PRACTICAL AND AESTHETIC REASONS, we're great believers in establishing three levels of light at the table: high, eye level, and low. Here, a sea of small votives provides a glow close to the table surface. Candles in hurricanes spaced out over the terrace serve as footlights and lend extra drama.

LIVING WITH HISTORY

LIKE SO MANY COMMUNITIES AROUND AMERICA, Charlotte is house-proud. We cherish our notable older homes and work to preserve our architectural heritage. This classically detailed Italianate house, with its stucco face and tile roof, offers a wonderful example of our local efforts in historic designation. Designed and built in 1917–18 by the celebrated Charlotte-based architect Louis H. Asbury (1877–1975) for Henry M. McAden, president of the First National Bank, and with extensive gardens originally laid out by Earle Sumner Draper, it presents itself to the street rather grandly. Its expansively proportioned light-washed rooms are equally impressive.

With a young family, our clients opted to renovate the interiors, making minimal structural changes because of the house's historic designation. We've worked to soften the architecture's inherent formality with comfortable, inviting furnishings and fabrics intended for everyday use.

In the capacious, double-height entry hall, viburnum and hellebores from the garden add a lovely, fresh touch. The viburnum that provided the blooms is original to the house and, at almost a hundred years old, still flowers gloriously.

A breathtakingly beautiful Colonial Revival double-horseshoe stairway frames the grand entrance hall. An antique Oushak lends softness and infuses the neutral palette with a wash of vibrant color; a crystal chandelier overhead adds sparkle.

To emphasize the symmetry, we flanked the entry hall with gilded, marble-topped French consoles under matching scenic panels painted by Terry Reitzel. We love the juxtaposition of the raw, unframed canvases and the much dressier furniture. Resting under each console is an Italian hand-carved horse-hoof bench.

As tempting as it may be to overfill large rooms, it's important to create negative space so that the eye has an opportunity to rest and appreciate what it's going to see next.

With windows and openings on all four sides and very generous proportions, the ground-floor rooms posed a challenge for creating comfortable, functional seating groups and providing the proper amount of lamp lighting for nighttime use. In the living room, a sisal rug and linen and cotton upholstery fabrics offset the formality of silk curtains and fine French antiques.

On one living room wall, a period trumeau mirror hangs over an antique French settee upholstered in a contemporary cotton weave. A stone-topped iron coffee table grounds this seating area. Pillows in soft greens and blues infuse the neutral room with soothing color.

Curtain panels of duck-egg-blue silk hang at the living room windows. The original grillwork and the dado detailing add a wonderful, subtle bit of pattern and definition to the room. A French eighteenth-century barometer surmounts an antique painted bergère dressed casually in cotton damask.

The primary ground-floor rooms are arranged in enfilade along the house's front, which creates a wonderfully balanced floor plan. Flanking the entry hall through 10-foot-wide doorways are the living room and dining room. Both have one long wall of windows and a fireplace at the far terminus; both open onto matching sunporches. To create continuity from room to room, we painted each the same creamy off-white—a lovely background on which to layer—and used sisal on the floors.

Our clients are true Francophiles when it comes to furniture. She's also collected some very beautiful art and mirrors, which these rooms show off to perfection. To make sure that the whole family could—and would—really live in every room of the house, we supplemented her antiques with comfortable, inviting upholstery covered in the kind of natural fabrics that exemplify everyday elegance. We also expanded our palette of neutrals with pale tones— duck-egg blues in the living room and soft, watery greens in the dining room.

One of the ground-floor rooms is the study, with original built-in bookcases and French doors that open to a back terrace. When we began our work, the original mahogany paneling was still in place, although it was obscured by layers of varnish. We had the varnish stripped down and the mahogany polished to a rich glow. An Oushak with beiges and browns warms the floor; that repetition of neutral tones creates a link between the different spaces.

An antique bronze and crystal chandelier hangs over the Louis XVI-style dining table. We used the slightly rougher backside of a silk damask to upholster the French-style dining chairs. Along the window wall is an antique Swedish bench.

As complementary colors, green and purple make each other more vibrant—hence the lavender accents here. We use damask frequently because we think it provides rooms with a classical base and historical reference.

Twin sunrooms, almost perfect cubes in dimension, bookend the ground floor. Any room with windows and doors on all four sides creates interesting opportunities when it comes to furniture placement.

The sunroom's original green tile flooring and light fixtures could not be changed. Sisal on top of the tile is a link to the other rooms; an antique Oushak on top of the sisal consolidates the seating area by the fireplace.

A neutral background creates a canvas for layering the beautiful objects that you love, the art and furnishings that you respond to, and the accessories and accent colors that make the room work for you.

COLOR PALETTES

EVERY DESIGNER HAS A MULTITUDE OF MEANS at his or her fingertips to create visual interest. We generally use neutral tones and soft colors to create a flattering backdrop for beautiful furniture, interesting textures, and wonderful objects and art. We have found that tranquil palettes allow for flexibility when it comes to changing the elements of a room, as we all inevitably do over time. And perhaps because we spend our days immersed in pattern and color, we like to give our eyes a rest when we come home. That naturally translates to what we do for our clients.

WE APPROACH THE PALETTE differently depending on the room's function. For the more heavily used spaces, like living rooms and family rooms, we like to create quieter backgrounds. We also love to work with historic paint colors, even when we're just applying a shade of off-white to the walls. Certain historic paint colors from certain brands have an almost translucent softness that infuses a room with a subtle but palpable atmosphere, one that changes character with the light over the course of the day.

THIS IS NOT TO SAY THAT WE NEVER USE SATURATED hues or specialty paint treatments; we do. But we all react emotionally to color, so we save the effects of strong color for the rooms that are less heavily trafficked. The dining room, for example, takes naturally to intense hues. It's an occasion space—even a theater of sorts. And what is more enchanting or dramatic than a color-drenched dining room in candlelight?

WHEN WE USE SATURATED COLORS, we're extremely selective. We tend to stay at the warm end of the spectrum, and we opt for shades that make sense in the context of the home's location. For a house at the beach, we might choose a gorgeous, glowing apricot-melon-colored glaze and curtains to match; a room like that will change its temperament, charmingly, from hour to hour and season to season. In Charlotte, on the other hand, we might go with a deeply saturated shade of yellow.

WE LIKE TO CREATE BOLDER EFFECTS in powder rooms and guest bedrooms. Because we use these rooms less frequently, we feel they can benefit from an extra punch of color or pattern. It's fun to offer a guest room with an unexpected bit of pizzazz.

In the master bedroom, a color palette of yellows, taupes, and grays soothes the senses. A plain taupe cotton lines the taupe-trimmed yellow silk bed hangings; upholstering the headboard is a cotton damask in pale taupe and grays. The ormolu sconces (opposite) are original to the house and flank an antique French mirror.

In the master bath, a French-style double-sink vanity is designed to look like a piece of furniture. Custom trumeau mirrors conceal twin medicine cabinets. The master bedroom fireplace (opposite) retains its original mantel.

SUBTLETY AND SURPRISE

HOW IS IT THAT WE FALL HEAD OVER HEELS for one house and not another? Sometimes the choice feels like a foregone conclusion. At other times, it seems more of a mystery—as certainly it must have when, a few years ago, our empty-nest clients acquired this romantic four-bedroom house on a rise inspired by elements of the English Tudor and Jacobean styles. The couple had always lived in (and loved) Georgian-style symmetrical red-brick homes, with very formal, very dressy public rooms at the front and family living quarters at the back. This house couldn't be more different. Designed by Ruard Veltman, a Charlotte-based architect, and constructed of limestone, plaster, and wood, it is full of carefully planned twists and turns, subtle architectural intrigue, and visual surprises. With living space on three floors, several exterior rooms, and beautiful landscaping, it hosts large affairs comfortably and in great style. For a spacious house, it also offers many different areas for two to be content. And that's precisely how they use it: for philanthropic events and for their own solitude.

The architectural details take their cue from the English Tudor and Jacobean styles, although there's not a half-timbered wall anywhere in sight. At the front entry, detailed limestone layers frame a coffered wood front door.

We like subtle finishing details—moss fringe, contrast welting, and tape. In the entry (opposite) an oriel bay window with leaded glass and dark muntins set into limestone provides a modern take on a classic architectural device, adding a note of history and a European sensibility.

So often, our design decisions respond directly to architecture. Here, the lime-washed pecky cypress ceiling, vast limestone fireplace, plaster walls, and leaded windows create an accommodating environment for elegant furnishings and accessories.

The living room seats at least ten people comfortably. The antique Oushak provided the basis for the color palette, and a spring-blooming ground cover outside inspired the pillow colors. Silk, velvet, cotton, and linen fabrics balance texture, matte, and sheen. The chandelier is gilt over wood with crystal.

The living room adjoins the dining room. Because it's a place where groups linger before moving to another area, we have left plenty of open space for people to move around.

We mixed furniture styles and periods for variety and included many small pieces for repositioning when necessary. The English Chippendale chair sits with a French bouillotte table and a stone column base that serves as a side table. The stools, coffee table, lamp, and settee are Italian. Over the mantel is a painting by Eric Aho.

꩜ *In the main salon (opposite), orchids bloom in the walnut jardiniere.*
A framed tapestry covers the powder room door. Among our favorite details are pillows
with mitered corners, nailheads, and trims.

This house has wonderful architectural nuances.
We really felt that if we filled it with too much pattern
and ornament, we would detract from its structural
beauty and the very elements—curved walls,
archways, leaded windows, beamed ceilings, and so
on—that we wanted to let shine.

This house doesn't give up its secrets all at once, which is a great part of its charm. Ruard says there are little design devices that beckon people from one area into the next. Changes of level on the ground floor contribute an element of surprise, as does the way windows frame unexpected vistas. The materials palette concentrates grander elements, such as carved limestone and plaster, in more public areas in the front of the house and warmer components, such as wood, in the more private areas.

From our point of view, designing these rooms was a wonderful opportunity. Our goal was to create multiple places and different types of spaces, both inside and outside, where two people could spend time together and enjoy themselves. The clients didn't want any part of the interior to feel too dressy, too stuffy, or too formal.

We made a conscious decision to use a background palette of neutral tones throughout the house to allow for color and contrast in accessories and artwork. The furnishings are a mix of European periods and styles, from French and Italian to English and Belgian. With the textiles, we emphasized texture above all and stuck almost entirely to natural fibers and materials.

The living room and dining room are one large area.
The Spanish-style dining room table seats ten when extended.

No matter what the scale, entertaining at home should never be overwhelming. When you have what you need within easy reach, you will always be prepared for any eventuality.

PREPARATION

THE TRUTH IS THAT NOTHING SPOILS a festive atmosphere like an anxious host. And nothing diminishes anxiety more and encourages spontaneity better than preparation. In entertaining at home as in so much else in life, forethought, consideration, and planning are key. That's why we believe that making sure our clients are well prepared for entertaining is a significant aspect of our job as designers.

WHEN THE ESSENTIALS—linens, place mats, stemware, flatware, candles and votives, etc.—are well organized and close at hand, whether in a separate storage area or just a drawer in the kitchen or pantry, it's much easier to feel relaxed about having people over, even at short notice. When you have what you need and you know what you have, planning for most occasions becomes a pleasure. You become comfortable with your options. You have a keen sense of the colors, shapes, patterns, and textures you like and how to put them together to create a charming table setting. You may not necessarily repeat the same components over and over again, but you give yourself the choice of continuity. Once you have that and the confidence that comes with it, improvising becomes much easier and much more fun.

EVERYONE APPRECIATES IT when attention is paid, but no one likes to feel the effort behind the scenes. When the table is ready ahead of time, everything looks and feels effortless. If you are preparing the meal yourself, try to do as much as you can and attend to as many of the last details as possible before your guests arrive so that you can relax and spend time with them instead of fussing in the kitchen. Remember: your goal is to be a guest at your own party. When your guests see you, interact with you, and know you're enjoying yourself, they relax and enjoy themselves too.

WE LOVE GOOD FOOD, but it's important to remember that the food is never the be-all and end-all of a special evening. You can keep the food comparatively simple. Not every dish needs to be elaborate, complicated, or fussy; one star is enough. But here's why we advocate the power of presentation so strongly: if you haven't had the time to cook as you might like or if it's a last-minute invitation, as long as you arrange the food on handsome serving pieces, set a lovely table with a pleasing palette, and light lots of candles, it will be a special evening no matter what. Add a few sprigs of something you've picked from your garden in a glass or a vase (either is fine from our point of view), or create a centerpiece of fruits or vegetables (pears or pomegranates, for instance, or artichokes or gorgeous eggplants in a range of colors) and voilà!

WHEN IT COMES TO ENTERTAINING, our hope is that if you're prepared, you won't stand on ceremony. When you want to see your friends and you don't have time to cook, takeout favorites are just fine—better when they're beautifully presented! You can always offer Klondike Bars for dessert. What's more fun, delicious, and memorable than that?

Our clients love to dine in different areas of the house as the mood takes them. The kitchen offers several possibilities, including the island, a long table for family dining and, up several steps, a family lounge with a large fireplace.

The kitchen works for both casual and catered affairs. The leather bar stools are on casters and nestle up easily to the island. Each seats two people, so four people can pull up to the counter at any one time.

An arrangement of dogwood branches is a lovely sign of spring. The custom banquette (opposite) stretches 12 feet from end to end. The high-backed English chairs add a necessary vertical element.

Tucked around a corner
and down several steps,
this lounge is one of the
house's unexpected—
even secret—spaces. The
expansive gas fireplace
with ceramic cannonballs
contains a window that is
visible from the drive.

Intended for winter use, this room
features paneling stained dark cordovan
and green, heavy flannel drapes, and
comfortable deep leather chairs and
ottomans for lounging by the fire. The
tooled leather side chair is an English
servant's chair. The table is French.

In the family room, we arranged lots of comfortable upholstered seating around an oversize ottoman. Ottomans are practical and multifunctional: you can put trays or stacks of books on them (this one has a shelf underneath for extra storage) or use them for footrests or extra seating.

In the master bath, we softened the sleek effect of the white marble and chrome with an antique Oushak and sheer wool curtains. Painted to match the walls, the custom-made bureau provides extra storage space for linens and toiletries.

The master bedroom (previous spread) has an enormous window seat. We put the shades on remote control so that they are easy to raise and lower. A floating wall separates the bedroom from a large lounge area. In the master bath, the mirror over the sink (right) slides to conceal the medicine cabinet; its twin is on the opposite wall.

On the covered porch, we kept the furniture clean-lined and simple to contrast with the swooping roof and arched enclosure. The chair frames and tabletop are mahogany, stained dark to match the beams and the trim. The custom swing is like a backless daybed.

With easy access to the kitchen, the covered outdoor dining area is yet another convenient spot for alfresco entertaining. The furniture is designed for exterior use. It remains outside all year; the seat cushions are covered in durable, pretty, easy-to-clean outdoor fabric.

The Belgian table has a slate-slab top with a raked edge; the base is vintage, with an elegant rusticity. The centerpiece is a candle altar once used on a church floor. The perfect height for dining, it adds a touch of drama for nighttime entertaining.

EUROPEAN INFLUENCES

WITH RESTRICTION AND DESIRE, YOU GET A FEVERISH ENGINE OF DESIGN, says architect Bobby McAlpine. He couldn't have expressed the story of our house more succinctly or poetically. About twenty years ago, when my husband and I had begun to think about how we wanted to live after our then-high-school-age children had finished college, we decided to build a smaller house where we could exist comfortably on one floor. We found a lot that we loved in one of Charlotte's gracious older neighborhoods. At 65 feet across and 120 feet deep, though, it was so skinny that we wondered whether we could possibly put a house on it. My sister in Alabama suggested that we consult Bobby, who was then starting to make quite a name for himself and his Montgomery-based firm, now McAlpine Tankersley Architecture. He came to visit, and he convinced us that we could squeeze something wonderful into the limited space. That's how we became fast friends.

Bobby McAlpine says that the design challenge for the Smiths' house was to create sequence and grandeur within "no width whatsoever." His pronounced axial plan establishes a clear procession and helps get light into the interior from all sides.

We wanted the house to look like it was transplanted from Europe. Bobby's design developed from three pairs of antique Belgian doors sitting in my warehouse; he used the doors' surrounding archway as a subtle architectural theme.

We knew we wanted a beautiful, interesting house, one where we would use every last inch. Bobby developed an asymmetrical back-to-front, upside-down plan to fit the house onto the lot and to accommodate our wish to live primarily on one level. With no room for a driveway or a garage at the back, we enter and exit the house through the front door, which I love. The stucco in the entry hall provides a nice transition from indoors to out.

The main living areas—a combined family/living room, the kitchen, and the adjacent breakfast area—are at the rear. We don't have a proper dining room, but for more formal dinners and special occasions, we can set a table at the base of the stairs. Our master bedroom is on the ground floor, as is the library. The three bedrooms upstairs come in handy for our two children and their families and for visiting friends. There's a dining terrace off the living room and a small garden that makes the most of the limited space.

Bobby calls the style of the house "country French come to town," which is exactly the spirit we had in mind. My love of England and France and my passion for antiques prompted our choice of materials, details, colors, and furnishings. I asked him to incorporate three pairs of Belgian doors that I'd had for a while; they provided the defining architectural theme of the archway, which recurs subtly throughout the interior.

When we entertain, which we do often, we tend to have small gatherings and the house flows easily. We just close the kitchen door and people come to rest in the living areas at the back of the house.

One set of antique Belgian doors encloses the kitchen; another, the living room.

I love antiques, and I prefer to have just a few really pretty, unusual things. They don't have to be priceless as long as they're unique and have some intrinsic value to them.

We spend most of our time in the living room, which has a TV and is large enough for three sofas. The stained cypress ceiling warms up the room, as does the fireplace. A sisal rug, which is so durable and casual, comes in handy with two dogs and six grandchildren.

Dressed in mohair and trimmed with nailheads and fringe, the large ottoman
in the living room can do double duty as a place to set a tray or for extra seating. The striped
horsehair fabric on the armchair (opposite), epitomizes sturdy elegance.

What's more compelling than beautiful wood worked to perfection by an artist of another era? Antiques bring history and soul with them wherever they go, and our favorite pieces definitely stand the test of time.

ANTIQUES

WE TRULY APPRECIATE FINE ANTIQUE FURNISHINGS and consider ourselves privileged to work with them, but we also find that antiques needn't be so fine in order to have a positive impact. Every antique from the most rustic to the most refined has a charm and a romance that makes it appealing and a decorative value that enhances a room. We've found that seventeenth-, eighteenth-, or nineteenth-century furniture and accessories from the European countries and the British Isles work well together in the same room, as long as there are some clean-lined contemporary things to provide balance.

EVERY ROOM NEEDS AT LEAST ONE SPECIAL PIECE to make it distinctive and to give it personality. That piece doesn't have to be an antique, but in our rooms it often is. Jane and I are drawn to unusually pretty pieces of old furniture and accessories. We believe that gorgeous brown wood with the patina of age or an interesting painted piece adds the kind of warmth, depth, and touch to a room that nothing else can.

BECAUSE WE'VE WORKED WITH ANTIQUES for so many years, we find that we look for pieces that are truly out of the ordinary, whether they're painted, gilded, embellished with marquetry or inlay, or just dressed in their original varnish or wax finish. Our preference is for exceptional wood and uncommon hardware, as well as the little things that make a piece unique—a compelling foot, a gorgeous leg, a lilting curve on the top. When a table, chest, sideboard, settee, or bookcase is really outstanding, it can become the starting point for an entire room. That's exciting, because that kind of inspiration can give you a very clear idea of what the room will look like in the end.

WE LOVE ANTIQUE TEXTILES AND RUGS, particularly Oushaks, and we use them often. Their muted palettes and delicate patterns suit our sensibility, and the older, handwoven fabrics lend such refinement and culture to a room. Antique mirrors are among our favorite accessories, because what's more wonderfully decorative on a wall than a fantastically carved antique frame fitted with an old mirror? The softly silvered glass lends a subtlety and luminosity to the reflection. And while the frames may not always have great value as antiques, they have tremendous decorative impact.

THERE'S SOMETHING WONDERFUL ABOUT ANTIQUE CHAIRS. Each is completely unique. They offer endless options. You can find one with the most funky little leg, another with something fabulous about the back, still another with a remarkable arm or cross-brace. We love to mix them, even around a dining table, just for variety and visual interest.

In the bar, above, a wonderful etching hangs between the cabinets. The kitchen (opposite), has a handy pass-through to the living room, and guests can pull stools up to the counter.

I enjoy cooking, and my kitchen is small but very functional, with two large pantries behind doors that flank the stove. I wanted it to be attractive—hence the snazzy stove that one of our designers says looks like a sports car and the quilted-stainless-steel refrigerator doors.

In the window bay at the base of the stairs, I keep a round table that can seat up to ten people.
We use it as a dining table or buffet, but usually it holds newspapers or books plus a container of flowers.

The interior is very well organized and well planned. The rooms are on an axis, and the adjacencies are natural. I love being able to see from room to room, and I appreciate that there's no wasted space.

The third set of antique Belgian doors encloses the library, which is on axis with the window bay at the base of the stairs across the front hall. Paisley pillows, a cord-trimmed ottoman covered in an old Aubusson rug, and leather upholstery create an atmosphere of warmth and welcome. Built-in shelves hold books and English and Chinese porcelains.

*We use the library much more in the wintertime than in the other seasons.
It's a kind of cocoon, with a fireplace and comfortable upholstery that suits us for reading, TV
watching, or gathering with friends. We also use it for dining on occasion.*

When we put a room together, we want it to be as beautiful in the future as it is right now. That's why we opt for designs with classic lines and natural fabrics in soft, neutral tones.

LASTING VALUE

WE WANT THE ROOMS WE DESIGN to have a timeless quality, to have what we call holding power. Slipcovers, pillows, and the occasional accessory aside, we don't change the elements of our surroundings all that often. We certainly don't update our interiors with the frequency we do our wardrobes. That is not to say that our rooms can't be fun and stylish. We just believe that the pieces we choose to live with—the individual components of our rooms— should be pieces with intrinsic value and enduring effect. The designs we select are designs we feel will abide, interest, and please the eye for the long term.

WHETHER YOU'RE INVESTING IN A PIECE of furniture or an entire room, it is important to look to the future. Both should be able to live softly over the years, and the only way they will is if they are built to last. Our sense of lasting worth lies at the heart of all our choices. We prefer materials that endure, clean lines, subtle backgrounds, understated patterns, and casual, comfortable upholstery dressed in neutral fabrics because we feel they age extremely well. We tend to use strong color and bold pattern sparingly.

DIFFERENT ROOMS REQUIRE DIFFERENT PIECES and palettes. Some rooms can be a little trendier, if that's your preference. A family room, for instance, can have fun pillows and a change of chair styles every so often. But when it comes to the basics, those elements like curtains or sofas meant to last for twenty years, we always try to keep the palette neutral.

SO MANY OF US TODAY ARE LIVING less formal lives than in the past, in rooms more cleanly styled. We want fabrics that we can wash or dry-clean at will, that are designed to take wear and tear, that are delightful to the touch and look good for the long term. Even when we opt for traditionally styled interiors, we tend to want our upholstery to have more streamlined shapes with the appropriate dressmaker details.

WE MAY PREFER QUIET PALETTES, upholstery, and plain, textured fabrics or those with understated pattern. But we also believe that rooms should be full of personality and express the people who live in them. Family pieces—silver, china, art, linens, and the occasional antique—do that wonderfully. So do collections of objects and accessories and keepsakes that are accumulated over the years.

NOTHING'S MORE HUMAN THAN GETTING swept up in the latest style or innovation. We do it too. But we suggest that when you have to have something trendy (and who doesn't?), don't go overboard. You can update your pillows or choose some elements for a fun table setting or something of that nature. That way, it won't be such a significant investment that you'll feel obligated to live with it for the next twenty years (when you'll tire of it much sooner).

The backyard contains a pool as well as a small garden that is pretty and easy to maintain. The dining porch is just outside the living room, tucked under the roof's overhang.

A marble slab tops the outdoor dining table. Hanging overhead is a wrought-iron chandelier with votives. It's lovely and wonderfully romantic, which makes up for the fact that it takes a bit of work (and patience) to light.

CLASSICAL COMFORTS

WHATEVER THE STYLE OR PERIOD OF ARCHITECTURE AND DECORATION, the most gracious homes flow from one room to another, from indoors to outdoors, in a way that feels as natural and effortless as breathing. This beautifully scaled Georgian Colonial, which the Charlotte-based architect Martin E. Boyer designed and built in the 1920s, epitomizes that kind of elegant, easy circulation.

The English-inflected architecture of the house, which is ringed by an embrace of terrace rooms, a landscaped pool area, an orangery, and a two-bedroom guesthouse, certainly reminds our clients of their English roots. It suits this family perfectly too, thanks to a recent renovation that brought it up to date to meet the family's needs.

With young children and a bustling menagerie, our clients desired a comfortable, elegant home with a sense of tradition. Our goal was to create rooms that support and enhance the constant hum of activity and frequent entertaining that form the core of their family lifestyle.

She is both an animal lover and a gardener of great skill and charm, as this little vignette of French hand-carved stone birds and a magnolia cut from the garden suggests.

The lunette's intricate fretwork repeats in the windows that flank the doors.
The library under the stair (opposite) is a family retreat; the stair riser detailing is original. In the
entry, an arrangement of garden peonies provides a burst of color atop an Italian commode.

Well-proportioned rooms, well-positioned windows,
and subdued but elegant ornamental detailing
are a few of the architectural intangibles that profoundly
enhance a home's atmosphere.

When these clients called, they had just begun a major renovation to update the kitchen, the children's bedrooms and baths, and the master bedroom and bath. Their goal was to improve the interior flow while retaining the classical organization of the floor plan so that they could truly enjoy every room in the house. That classicism begins at the front door, where a spacious central entry hall welcomes people and beckons them further into the interior. Flanking the stairwell is a living room that opens to an outdoor dining terrace and an outdoor room with a fireplace; under the stair is a library that opens onto the same terrace. To the other side of the hall is a formal dining room and, through a passageway, an expanded kitchen intended for everyday family living, with plenty of space for the children to gather with their friends and to do their homework.

The lovely proportions of the interior rooms, the understated ornament of the original architectural detailing, and the wash of daylight through the house from dawn to dusk are elemental intangibles that ensure comfort. A particularly attractive architectural feature of this house is that each room on the rear perimeter has a door to the exterior, which allows the children and the adults to move easily between indoors and out.

Panels of a cotton and linen abstract damask hang at the living room windows;
the strié finish on the walls is a deeper shade of wheat than that of the entry hall.
Sisal on the floor completes the tonal palette.

The living room (previous spread) accommodates three seating groups; a curtain-framed doorway (opposite) leads to an outdoor dining terrace. In the powder room (above), Johannes Kip's antique etchings of garden views hang on walls covered with hand-painted paper.

*The formal dining room plays a significant
role in the life of this family and this house, as its
appointments make very clear.*

The English country house style—with its multiple layers of history and generational heritage—is this family's tradition. They came to us with a collection of pieces, including the wonderful ancestral portraits on the dining room walls, a glorious collection of silver, some of which we display on the dining room sideboard, and a few larger heirloom items, such as the case clock that stands guard at the entrance to the dining room.

At the room's center is an antique English dining table; with leaves, it extends to seat twenty. Surrounding it are oval-back chairs upholstered in a wheat-colored linen that complements the walls and trimmed with tape accents and nailheads for a subtle flair. Providing storage on opposite walls are an eighteenth-century French chiffonade and an antique George II English sideboard. To warm the room and provide a wonderful glow in candlelight, we painted the walls with Farrow & Ball's Print Room Yellow, which also provides a beautiful backdrop for the family portraits. The quilted curtains at the window and the sisal underfoot inject a subtle textural note that contrasts pleasantly with the many polished surfaces.

*A gilt and iron chandelier hangs elegantly over the dining room table. Polished to
a high sheen, the mahogany table (following spread) reflects etched crystal glasses, monogrammed napkins,
gleaming silver candlesticks, and garden bouquets—a setting of quiet drama.*

Nothing should ever be so precious that you cannot use it. Beauty is functional, and it uplifts us all. A silver spoon and a fine porcelain cup transform a simple cup of tea into a memorable moment and an everyday luxury.

EVERYDAY LUXURIES

ONE OF OUR GUIDING DESIGN PRINCIPLES is that beauty is both functional and practical. Many of the things we value were meant to play a role in the daily acts of living—to elevate the everyday. That's why we want to bring them out of the drawer or off the basement shelf and into the light of day. Silver is a perfect example. Whether it's your wedding silver, the flatware you inherited from your mother, or the tea service you cherish from your grandmother, use it. It's the better for it, and so are you. You can set a tray in your bathroom with a hand towel and a special bar of soap. You can put a salver on your bedside table with a bottle of water and a lovely crystal glass. You even can place a silver pitcher in a wicker basket, if you like; that combination of the casual and the fine is so contemporary and a sly twist on the contrast of high and low. You needn't display every piece of your service, and certainly spread out select pieces throughout your rooms. But smaller components, like your creamer and sugar bowl? Why not leave them on a tray on the kitchen counter? Whenever you see them or use them, they will brighten your day and remind you of happy times and people whom you love.

WHEN WE FIRST STARTED GOING TO ENGLAND years ago, we were amazed by the way the English use their fine things to elevate every occasion, even a simple cup of tea. Searching for antiques in the middle of the English countryside, we might find ourselves wandering into a farmhouse in hot pursuit of some elusive piece of furniture. The farmer and his wife would offer tea, of course. They'd bring it out on a tray with a nice porcelain cup and a silver spoon—even when we were in boots in the muck. That memory is priceless, but so is the lesson it taught us about the importance of using the things we have.

SILVER FLATWARE IS MEANT FOR USE. Designed to serve a purpose, it is a tool of the highest order. It also feels divine in the hand. We often advise our clients to keep their silver utensils—their beautiful knives, forks, and spoons—in containers on the kitchen counter, like a bouquet. You can make a bouquet from a collection of any number of beautiful things, and, like a bouquet of flowers, that massing of loveliness will add something special to the room. A pretty silver bowl has the same effect, especially if it's filled with something tasty—pistachios or nuts or candy or whatever. Just remember to put it out of reach of the dog!

Design is as much about creating feelings as it is about enhancing function. Some rooms are meant for calmness and hush, others for excitement. When we put a room together, we always have an emotion in mind.

The library walls are upholstered in the same soothing blue linen that we used for the curtains. The consistency of color creates a quiet, contemplative environment.

Much of this family's life occurs in this combined kitchen and family room, which is designed for the everyday wear and tear that comes with a house full of children. Flanking cabinets store linen, china, glasses, and flatware.

144

Kitchens are the heart of today's home, particularly when the home is alive with the activities of young people. We've made sure that there is plenty of space for the children to do their homework and easy access to the backyard. The window bay with dining table creates an invitation for family and friends to gather casually.

A major feature of the renovation was the expansion of the kitchen/family room area into a casual, comfortable, multifunctional space. For this family, that means pets too: the dogs and cats have full run of the house.

The need for durability and easy cleaning always brings function to the fore, but for us aesthetics are equally important. Fortunately, there are many fabrics in the market today that serve both purposes. Faux leather, for instance, has come a very long way from the leather look-alikes of years ago: it's hard-wearing, good-looking, pleasant to the touch, and easily wiped down when a drink spills, a claw drags, or crumbs drop. We used it to cover the bar stools that pull up to the island, and it's worn beautifully with everyday use. On the English chairs around the dining table is a cotton check that we had treated and finished for easy care. To surface the countertops and island, we used Calcutta marble; the warm white stone wears wonderfully. An antique painted wood and iron chandelier over the table and curtains with embroidered borders add layers of elegant detail. Underfoot are radiant-heated Peacock Pavers to provide warmth when needed.

All the rooms in this house have wonderful views of the gardens.

Master bedrooms are our private retreats, the places we go to recharge ourselves. As the first and last room we see each day, we believe they can—and should be— wonderfully restorative.

In the master bedroom, a loveseat at the bed's foot is useful for TV watching. A strié paper covers the walls; at the windows are curtains of cream-colored silk. The renovation opened up his and hers dressing rooms and baths.

The family built his and hers baths and dressing areas into the eaves.
Hers contains a bathtub with an oval window (opposite) and a walk-in shower.

By the back door, symmetrically placed lockers house the children's sports equipment and shoes. Using cuttings from the gardens, floral designer Jay Lugibihl has assembled a bouquet of dried alliums, grasses, Swiss chard, and branches of Japanese maple.

We all tend our gardens in our own way.
The fresh-cut flowers, potted blooms, and greenery brighten
our lives—and our rooms—beyond measure.

FLOWERS

IN THE SOUTH, we enjoy the four seasons. Because of our temperate Southern climate, we have numerous species that contribute to a year-round bloom cycle. We both love flowers, and we cannot image our lives, our homes, and our rooms without them.

WE PREFER UNSTUDIED ARRANGEMENTS, and we love to fill our rooms with whatever happens to be at the peak of its beauty at the given moment. Our floral designer, Jay Lugibihl, is a master at surveying a garden, seeing what nature provides, and taking advantage of it to create moments of beauty throughout the home.

MANY OF OUR CLIENTS have well-established gardens with wonderful plants for cutting. When Jay heads out of doors to gather the materials for his still lifes, we marvel at what he finds and how he manages to arrange his armful of cuttings in ways that look effortless and personal.

EVERY BLOOM, BRANCH, AND GRASS that adds color to the rooms of this house comes from its garden. The cuttings include 'Annabelle' hydrangea, garden roses, lamb's ear, and gardenia, plus the boxwood placed throughout the house.

FOR EVERYDAY, WE PREFER SIMPLE FLOWER ARRANGEMENTS. We find it refreshing when they feel easy and relaxed. It's not necessary to overstuff your vessels or to overdo the flowers in a room. A magnolia blossom or a single camellia in a glass or bud vase on the bedside table can bring a smile and help us begin and end the day with one of nature's wonders.

THE TYPE OF OCCASION DETERMINES the style of the floral arrangement. If you are hosting a seated dinner, lower flowers allow people to make eye contact and to converse across the table. If the dinner is a buffet, a larger, grander arrangement adds a note of drama. Choose colors that go with the season and the decor: in the fall, for instance, you might work with persimmons, rose hips, and maple leaves, and perhaps a pomegranate or two. Foliage is also always an option: boxwood, aucubas, and all sorts of evergreens make a fine base for the arrangement and are beautiful on their own as well.

JAY SAYS THAT WHEN HE CAN GATHER everything from the client's yard and create something glorious and unique, that's the beauty of nature. We think it's art too.

When a house opens up naturally to the outdoors, as this one does, we like to make the most of the connection. For exterior rooms, even those with a roof, it's important to select furnishings and fabrics that are comfortable, durable, and weather resistant.

The dining terrace outside the living room merges into a lattice-framed seating area with an outdoor fireplace that's just beyond the library door. A mirror atop the mantel reflects the garden. The rattan sofas are upholstered with indoor/outdoor fabrics for durability.

KINSHIP WITH
THE LAND

MY HUSBAND AND I LOVE THE AMERICAN WEST with its spectacular vistas, remarkable wildlife, and breathtaking cycle of seasons. When we found this property in Jackson Hole, Wyoming, we decided to build a retreat where we could gather our family and entertain our friends. We envisioned a house that would be one with the landscape, with inviting public spaces and great private areas too. The Bozeman, Montana–based architecture firm of Jonathan L. Foote & Associates created that place for us here. We call it Four Deer Ranch.

Jonathan and his partner Paul Bertelli practice architecture in the old-school manner: they are designer-builders who work closely with master craftsmen. Their preferred construction materials are beautiful century-old timbers and river rock. They honor the vernacular tradition of the region with houses that bow to the scale of their surroundings. This can mean, as it does here, that the living areas are spread out in a series of pavilions that connect to one another by glassed-in passageways that put you amid nature herself.

Designed by the firm of Jonathan L. Foote & Associates of Bozeman, Montana, landscaped by architect Jim Verdone, and constructed of old timber and Montana moss rock, the Schwabs' house seems at one with its Snake River site.

The house spreads its wings wide, and the rear overlooks a man-made trout pond and the mountains beyond. A timber planter (opposite), houses a selection of annuals, perennials, and indigenous grasses.

The house is sited with some reserve and partially obscured
by the aspen and cottonwood trees that surround it.
On arrival, it spreads out in a wide, welcoming embrace.

The house is handsome in size, yet it is designed to welcome, not to overwhelm. While the rustic nature of the old timber and river stone contributes to its friendliness, so does the way the house is laid out. Surrounded by native white-barked aspens, indigenous grasses, and other natural plantings, the structure is impossible to view in one glance as you approach. Even as you get closer, you can only glimpse parts of it through the trees. When you finally round the circular drive and pull up to the front door, it unfolds its wings and envelops you.

In the summer we have found that we live at the back of the house, where our outdoor rooms beckon us into the landscape. A terrace off the living room has a fire pit, which is a lovely place to gather for evenings of conversation and roasting marshmallows under the stars. A terrace off the kitchen has a covered dining porch where we love to share meals with family and friends.

The main house encompasses the double-height entry and living room, dining room, and mudroom, with bedrooms spread among the pavilions. The master area has its own pavilion, with the master bedroom, study, and his and hers bathrooms. Another houses a playroom area and two bedrooms, one on the ground level and one above. Still another houses a guest wing. A bunk room above the garage serves as an additional bedroom, which comes in handy, especially when we have a full house.

The double-height, stone-paved entry features a handcrafted stairway leading to a bedroom.

A suede-covered ottoman sits by the living room fireplace, with a low, hoof-footed, hide-covered stool nearby. An antique French chandelier hangs overhead; an elk rack surmounts the timber mantel. Natural linen curtains hang at the living room windows (opposite). The mix of fabrics also includes mohair, leather, and cotton herringbone.

In the dining room, an eighteenth-century Belgian table rests beneath an English ebony-and-inlaid-marble mirror and English reindeer rack. In the front hall (opposite), a Jane Rosen casein and ink on paper hangs over a painted chest flanked by wrought-iron sconces.

Succulents on the table and Ultrasuede napkins, above, bring the living room's soft green tones into the dining room. The silver antler candlesticks (opposite) are from Argentina. Naturally shed antlers also ornament the tabletop.

From the kitchen to the bedrooms to the passageways,
every space in the house offers magnificent
views of the surrounding landscape. We often feel
when we're here that the light is palpable.

Handcrafted elements, like Idaho artisan Clair Sharp's fantastic hand-hewn furniture, combine with more refined materials and finishes and a selection of antiques to create comfortable, cozy rooms filled with personality and patina. The color palette tends to my favorite soothing robin's egg and wildflower blues, tans, and soft, sage-y greens, all of which blend very beautifully with the outdoors.

The living room is flooded with natural light, and the huge picture window frames a spectacular view of the Tetons. The dining room is light-washed as well. Both rooms benefit from the presence of a fireplace. In these rooms, as throughout the house, textured fabrics invite the touch of the hand and reward that touch no matter the season. Natural linen curtains at the windows add a little bit more dimension. I have also worked in some vintage textiles as pillow covers; they just seem to suit the spirit of the house. The mix of natural textures with fragments that show their years works especially well in an environment like this one, with its river-rock and half-timber construction, great beams of old timber, and wide plank floors strewn with antique Oushaks and the occasional Turkish tulu rug.

Wrought-iron chandeliers and door hardware add yet another layer to the elegantly rustic elements. African baskets and my husband's collection of Native American beadwork infuse the guest rooms with personality. Old French wine bottles converted into lamps bring a subdued reflective element to certain rooms. As for the deer and reindeer racks and antlers, many of which we've collected from the woods, what could be more appropriate in a place called Four Deer Ranch?

The kitchen, which features cabinetry crafted of old timber, includes a dining area (following spread) with an oval table, a banquette, and a hand-hewn bench and stools.

If you're well prepared, well stocked, and set up for any eventuality, entertaining becomes so much more fun. That's why it's great to have a designated place for refreshments that's easy to reach and ready to go.

REFRESHMENTS

CINDY AND I BELIEVE THAT PREPARATION and presentation are two keys to great entertaining, whether it's an impromptu gathering or a seated dinner. Preparation involves planning, but it also involves design and organization. If you designate a place for your party things and refreshments, you'll always be able to put your hand on whatever you need when you need it most. If you've space for a separate bar area with storage, ice maker, refrigerator, sink, and so on, that's absolutely wonderful. If you don't, a well-stocked tray on a table or chest in your dining room or your living room will do beautifully.

WE BOTH PERSONALLY USE A LOT OF TRAYS. They're pretty, practical, and portable. If you have friends in for coffee, you can set up the coffee service on a tray, prepare the cup of coffee there, and take it to your guests. Or you can carry the tray with the coffee service to wherever you're planning to sit, set it on a table or ottoman nearby, and pour right there.

IF YOU HAVE A SEPARATE BAR AREA, you'll want to store glasses of all types. In addition to wine, champagne, and highball glasses, we like to stash a stack of plastic to-go cups on the shelves because they always seem to

come in handy. You might want to keep some acrylic glasses on the shelves too, because there are always small children who want to join the adults in a glass of lemonade from the bar. Whether you're offering apple juice, ginger ale, or perhaps a glass of milk, providing refreshments for the little ones is so much easier when you don't have to step away to the kitchen or the pantry for supplies.

YOU MAY NOT BE ABLE TO KEEP A FULL BAR on a tray, but you can have the specific things that you need for the moment. Glasses, an ice bucket, water, mixers—the choice depends on what you're serving. If you're having cocktails, you can compose the bottles and setups—lemons, limes, napkins, glasses, a bottle opener, a nice spoon—nicely on the tray.

IF YOU HAVE HOUSEGUESTS ARRIVING in mid or late afternoon, it's lovely to have a tray ready with a nibble and some ice water. If your guests are coming for a late-afternoon visit, it's just as nice to have a small snack— nuts, cheese straws, or olives—arranged with some napkins and a blossom or a green sprig in a glass or vase. Remember the power of presentation, and think of your cheese straws and napkins as a still life in the making. Every offering tastes better when it's presented in an appealing way.

A casual bouquet enlivens the bedside table in the master suite. Clair Sharp made the bed of lodgepole pine and topped the posts with finials made of Douglas fir branches collected from the woods.

In one bedroom (above) are handcrafted beds, a table, and a painting by Denver artist William Matthews. In another (opposite), part of my husband's treasured collection of Native American beadwork hangs above the upholstered headboard.

The mudroom (left) serves as the foyer in winter when snow piles at the front door. On top of the antique Oushak is one of our handmade tables, which holds a moose-rack planter. We store wood for the living and dining room fireplaces in the walkway (opposite) between the two rooms.

The mudroom entrance (above) comes in handy in the winter when the snowplow can't manage the circular front drive. Off the living room is a terrace with a fire pit (opposite), where we gather on chilly evenings for conversation and s'mores.

Within the image, the invitation reads:

SURVIVORS BRUNCH

SUNDAY, AUGUST 21ST

10:30 UNTIL 1:00

FOUR DEER

JACKSON HOLE

THE SCHWABS

R.S.V.P. TO JANE
704.004.3038
JBSCHWAB2005@YAHOO.CC

🍃 *The porch off the kitchen (opposite) makes outdoor dining easy. Around the custom-made table are twig chairs from the mountains of North Carolina. In the basket are cozy fleece capes, which we got in Botswana and which keep us warm for an early morning coffee or after the sun goes down.*

With a vertical railing on one side only, the bridge offers an unobstructed view of wildlife in the woods, the trout in the pond, and the mountain sunrises and sunsets. On warm afternoons, it's wonderful to sit on the edge and dangle your feet into the cool water below.

When we're on the bridge, we love to enjoy the captivating view of the mountains and the ever-changing light. For comfort, we always make sure to keep a throw or two handy.

CLOSE TO NATURE

THIS HOUSE IS MEANT TO BEAR SILENT WITNESS TO ITS ENVIRONMENT, says its architect, our friend Bobby McAlpine, of the Montgomery, Alabama, firm McAlpine Tankersley Architecture. Stone walls, a low-swooping cedar shake roof, and dark-painted trim help it do just that—beautifully. Sited on a steep hillside in the Carolinas' Blue Ridge Mountains, the three-bedroom home practically disappears into the landscape.

As is so often the case with houses designed by McAlpine Tankersley, the quality of the architecture profoundly influenced our decisions about the elements of interior design. How could it not? Under that shake roof nestle beautifully proportioned and detailed rooms, each oriented to frame and enhance the magnificent views, each enclosed by walls of wood and local stone. Our clients' discerning tastes, which we know well after designing other homes for them, helped lead the way.

Designed to merge into the mountainside, the house appears to skim the ground, especially from the rear drive, shown here. The dark-painted trim, stone walls, and cedar shake roof act as a most effective camouflage.

Natural, local materials, assembled and handcrafted by local artisans, imbue this mountain house with a palpable connection to its surroundings and a deep, abiding calm. What's more compelling than a cozy corner by a roaring fire?

Gracious, precise, and organized, this couple takes a very thoughtful, very selective approach to decorating. They invest great care in their homes, but they prefer to live in calm, comfortable, restrained surroundings unencumbered by an excess of things.

Entry to the house is from the rear drive through a generously wide screened doorway, where steps descend into the foyer. There, the palette of natural materials brings the exterior inside with a refined rusticity and a distinctive elegance. The hand-planed floors of the foyer are stained almost black. The walls throughout the house are white ash, pickled a soft gray with a hint of blue that subtly enhances the pattern of the grain.

Opening off the foyer is an enormous great room, a combined living and dining area that spans the width of the house and focuses on a bay that cantilevers out over the mountainside. Dark-stained hand-hewn beams overhead and dark-stained muntins around small windowpanes create a sense of gravity in the face of so much open space. At one end of the room is a massive hearth that is framed by a carved mantel of local limestone and placed into a wall of hand-set local stone. Where better to create a cozy corner just for two? And what draws the eye away from a beautiful view more compellingly than a fire? When this couple has the house all to themselves, as they often do, they find that they relax together in this "sitting room" in front of the fireplace, which is just as we designed. The chimney configuration affords them the extra convenience of stacking their cords of wood right up against the fireplace.

A Chinese wedding drum serves as a convenient table for sitting fireside.

At the front of the house, a wide bay projects over the mountainside. Dark-stained muntins help frame the spectacular view.

The palette of earth tones, blues, and grays washes quietly through the combined living and dining room, which opens onto a dining porch beyond. For textural contrast, we juxtaposed linens, cut velvet, and mohair with earthenware, glass, and hand-hewn wood and stone.

Very large rooms can overwhelm, which is why the furniture plan is so important. We strive to create intimate, inviting seating areas for two in addition to those arranged to welcome groups of four and more.

When we're developing furniture plans for multifunctional spaces as large as this one, we always try to include an intimate area for two in addition to comfortable, welcoming seating arrangements for larger groups. This great room, which measures approximately 30 feet by 40 feet and opens onto the kitchen, easily accommodates that intention. Here we've established three defined seating areas, plus adaptable space and a dining area at the end of the room that flows directly into the kitchen. At the other end of the room is the massive stone fireplace, framed by cozy seating for two.

As we begin our selection process for furnishings and accessories for any project, we always carefully consider its context, because we want the components of the room to feel natural and appropriate to the setting. Here, we opted for rustic yet elegant pieces that look as if they could have come from right here in the Blue Ridge Mountains, and perhaps in the case of some of the ceramic and stone accessories, even straight out of the earth. Atop one of the living room side tables is an arrangement of clay pots, with flowers and grasses plucked from their yard. Atop the dining table, there are three earthenware vessels with creamy glazes and forms that beg the touch.

Texture is everything in a great room such as this one, where the tradition of craft is present but quiet and understated. A hand-woven rug in brown and gray unfurls across the floor. The fabrics, so tactile, offer contrast for the eye and the hand—linen, mohair, cut velvet. In neutral blues, grays, and browns, they are also pleasing and peaceful.

The dining area (opposite) opens onto a porch with a beamed ceiling. An iron and wood table suits the setting.

In the library, serenity reigns. A smattering of art and objects adds layers of interest to the room, but the overall effect is one of calmness and restraint.

EDIT, EDIT, EDIT

AS SURPRISING AS THIS MAY SEEM FOR TWO PEOPLE who truly love beautiful things, we are careful to avoid clutter. Clutter defeats the intention of our work, which is to create comfortable, inviting, welcoming rooms that serve a purpose and are restful in spirit. That's why we are such great believers in the "edit, edit, edit" approach to design and decoration, and why we tend to take a hard line when it comes to blue-penciling our own and our clients' possessions.

EDITING IS A PROCESS, and it's a process that bears repeating on a regular basis for all the obvious reasons. It's not always easy to sort through our own possessions; we all get emotionally attached to our things. That's why we have found it very helpful to have a method underlying the decision-making process. Ours begins with: if it isn't functional, if it isn't beautiful, and if it has no sentimental value, let it go. Another consideration might be to put things away for a while and see if you miss them; if you don't, you can let them go as well. Our third piece of advice is just as classic: every now and then, step back and take a good, hard look at what you've accumulated and see what you can discard.

EDITING HELPS GIVE A ROOM A SENSE OF VISUAL RHYTHM. The eye needs places to rest between interesting pieces. Beautiful things also take on greater significance and purpose when they are fewer and far between. This is not to say we disapprove of collections; we don't. We think they're fantastic. But as much as we love collections, they can create a kind of visual cacophony when there are too many of them and they're not properly displayed. We have found that careful grouping is the key to keeping the eye delighted but not overwhelmed. If you do have a collection of something—whether it is pottery, exotic shells, or decorative boxes—we suggest you consider displaying the individual elements together as a family. When you're composing the arrangement, you might think about organizing it in terms of form, color, proportion, scale, pattern—in other words, as if it were a work of art. Bookshelves are a terrific place to do that, as are tabletops.

OUR INDIVIDUAL COMFORT LEVEL with clutter and the way each of us edits our possessions are highly personal matters. Some people love spare spaces. Other people feel more comfortable when they have many things around them. But if you love things as we do, we suggest you step back every so often and assess your surroundings—and then edit, edit, edit.

The kitchen's soapstone counters and sink are on different levels. Adjacent are a working pantry and a windowed breakfast nook with banquette seating and pull-up chairs in several sizes and styles, just for visual interest. Hanging over the workspace is an iron chandelier.

The ground-floor master bedroom overlooks the treetops. At the foot of the bed (opposite), an ottoman provides storage. A window bay in the bedroom contains a chaise for reading or lounging and her home office. When she wants to hide her desk, she simply draws the curtains.

In the powder room (left), the faucet and the sconce are set to one side; it's not the most common of arrangements, but it works beautifully within the confines of this room. The upstairs bath, which overlooks the roof beams of the porch below, features matching sinks

The screened porch off the dining room (opposite) is another great room for daily living and entertaining, with a huge fireplace, plenty of comfortable seating, and a dining area. The driveway pulls up to the tool shed by the back entrance.

CAPTIVATED BY LIGHT

THESE CLIENTS AND THEIR DAUGHTERS have long called Greenwich, Connecticut, home base. In recent years, though, they've been escaping to this lush Florida property for breaks from the worst of the northeastern winters. While they loved the house that was original to this site—a design by John Volk, one of the founding fathers of the Palm Beach vernacular—they realized after several years of living in it that it didn't suit their intentions for the long term. They and Thomas M. Kirchhoff, their Jupiter, Florida-based architect, considered every possible way to renovate the existing structure. Finally, they opted to start over.

The result? This magnificent, recently completed, light-washed Mediterranean-style residence in North Palm Beach. Among its many charms, it has striking views of the Atlantic Ocean, expansive and gracious rooms, a charming guesthouse, and an unusual trio of loggias.

The architect Thomas Kirchhoff specializes in contextually apt, beautifully detailed residences designed for today's lifestyles and distinguished by appropriate ornament inspired by Palm Beach's legendary architects: Addison Mizner, John Volk, Marion Syms Wyeth, and Maurice Fatio. The property unfolds harmoniously behind an intricately detailed front gate.

Creating a new house is an exciting, challenging, stimulating, and sometimes daunting collaborative process. The better you understand your preferences and the more clearly you can explain them, the happier you will ultimately be.

The experience of living in the original Volk-designed house, which had a spectacular loggia, taught our clients several important lessons about the Florida lifestyle. The first and foremost was, as they put it, "You want to live outside as much as possible." That said, they asked Tom to incorporate three loggias seamlessly into the overall design.

As the house continued to evolve in plan, the clients emphasized that they wanted it to function well, flow effortlessly, look lovely, and, most of all, maximize light and openness—all of which are inherent principles of Tom's architectural philosophy. They also opted to take advantage of the full extent of the lot, which, at 100 feet by 400 feet, presented some unusual constraints. The decision to sink the driveway below grade along the property line and place the guesthouse and the main house like parentheses at either end of the lot opened up the core of the property beautifully. Lush landscaping and a pool by landscape architect Mario Nievera now bridge the distance, and there's a wonderfully gracious procession of arrival from the front gate of the property through its full length to the gated front door of the main house.

On first entering the house, you feel the generosity of its volume; the pleasure of its natural materials palette of plaster, cast stone, limestone, pecky cypress, and other wood species; the graciousness of its architecture; and the specificity of its ornament from column capitals and ceiling beams to pilasters. Tom has quietly choreographed a strong sense of axiality, so it is possible to see from the entry hallway through to the living room and the ocean beyond.

Atop the foyer bureau, a blown-restoration-glass mirror reflects the front door, and a driftwood planter holds tropical foliage from the garden plus a few branches of quince.

A skirted central table in the foyer repeats the ceiling detail with dimensional exactitude. An eighteenth-century Italian gilt-on-wood lantern descends directly on point. In the entry hall (opposite), succulents nestle into old shells. Italian ring-cut crystal lamps flank an early nineteenth-century English mirror hanging above a marble-topped console.

When a house opens itself to such captivating surroundings as these, why compete? The color palette reflects the environment of sand, sea, sky, and garden, with gentle neutrals, soft blues, and warm accents.

In the light-filled, double-height living room, a serene blue-and-white palette reigns with a few azure splashes and melon accents. Hanging overhead is an antique Italian chandelier. On the walls flanking the entry archway are massive, early nineteenth-century mirrors originally from a chateau in Belgium, Tuscan-style painted buffets, and sconces, which add another level of light.

In the living room, an inlaid bone coffee table, a basket table, antique
Italian end tables with inlaid marble tops, and Italian ring-cut azure crystal lamps add
texture. The backgammon table suits the game-loving family.

Because of the scale of the architecture, we wanted to create an atmosphere of comfort and welcome throughout the house while keeping the rooms as open, light, and airy as possible.

When the family is here, they spend as much time as possible outside. For that reason, they had Tom create a loggia off the kitchen and family room. The dining room, glazed an entrancing shade of cantaloupe, is stylish enough to accommodate more formal evenings and friendly enough for breakfast on cool or raining mornings.

Their ground-floor master bedroom is an especially serene space. It features a white-painted four-poster bed, an array of comfortable seating, light-filtering sheers, and curtains detailed with crewel stitching and a linen band. The palest blue glaze covers the wall.

The living room is stunning, with stenciled 25-foot ceilings and leaded-glass clerestory windows. Two seating groups make for comfortable conversation and easy TV viewing.

Paneled in pecky cypress, his office/library can double as a guest bedroom if necessary. At the window overlooking the ocean, we placed his custom, Ultrasuede-covered desk. A mirror on the far wall reflects the ocean view to the room's occupants.

Upstairs is for the younger generation. The daughters' bedrooms capture spectacular views of the ocean. Adjoining is a lounge area for reading, watching TV, and gathering with friends; a convertible daybed provides additional sleeping capacity.

With an active family lifestyle, the basement exercise room gets a good workout. Also in the basement are a wine cellar and a home theater, which everyone uses far more than they first imagined.

In the gallery, lanterns and a stone floor with pebble inlays emphasize the rhythm of the groin vaults.

The cantaloupe-painted dining room has many moods. For a beautiful breakfast or lunch, quartz votives and hibiscus from the garden make for an easily arranged centerpiece; the painting is by Mary Heilmann. A scalloped marble planter filled with orchids and cantaloupe-colored votives (opposite) suit a dressier occasion. An iron and silver leaf chandelier glimmers overhead; unlined wool sheers filter the light beautifully.

The kitchen encompasses a casual seating area (above). Faux leather-covered bar stools pull up to the island counter under the beamed ceiling. Charlotte-based kitchen and millwork specialist Emily Bourgeois consulted with us on the kitchen; her wonderful design includes the custom copper hood and recessed cabinets set into a tile wall.

We believe that function and comfort are closely related. In the lounge area between the daughters' bedrooms, the sectional seating arrangement is cozy and inviting. It also converts to extra sleeping quarters when the need arises.

Upstairs are two bedrooms for the couple's daughters and an adjoining lounge area where the girls and their friends can gather and watch TV. The comfy sectional sofa can do double duty as an extra bed or two when there's overflow; washable linen upholstery makes for easy maintenance.

Design is not just a matter of aesthetics.
Our goal is to create homes that are
comfortable, functional, and inviting, and that
automatically put people at ease.

COMFORT COMES FIRST

COMFORT MEANS DIFFERENT THINGS to different people. For us, comfort is a practical matter. Like every other aspect of design, it involves careful analysis and planning.

EVERY ROOM HAS DIFFERENT REQUIREMENTS for comfort. Once you know the purpose(s) of a room, you can decide what pieces of furniture you need and how best to arrange them. In a room where your children are going to watch TV, for instance, you'll need a maximum amount of seating. That's the room where you might want to put an oversize sofa. The children can flop on it, and you can join them. If your room is a family room for adults, on the other hand, you'll need sofas and enough chairs so that you can gather your friends together to watch a movie or a sports event. You'll also want convenient places—that is, side and coffee tables—to set drinks and lamps.

EACH OF US HAS OUR OWN COMFORT ZONE depending on our physical needs and preferences. We ask our clients what type of seating they like. Do they need a deep sofa? Or would they prefer a shallow seat? Do they like firm or soft cushions? Those questions and their answers are how we communicate about comfort.

WHEN IT COMES TO BALANCING sitting comfort and maintenance, each of us has distinct priorities. Some people don't want to fluff and plump cushions, and other people are happy to do it. If your clients have several children or grandchildren who are going to be all over the furniture and they don't want to fix back cushions all the time, we recommend a tight back so the sofa stays neat.

A CUSHION IS AN INVITATION TO SIT, STAY, AND ENJOY. We often use fully upholstered chairs around the dining room table for that reason. We like upholstered club chairs that swivel and chairs that are on casters so they're easy to move. One of our favorite styles is an extra-wide upholstered bar stool on casters, a two-seater that can pull up to the kitchen counter or the kitchen island. Ottomans, benches, and low, upholstered stools can provide extra seating and/or a place to prop your feet. Little chairs are fun: children love them, and adults enjoy them too. As for the style of upholstery or slipcovers, sometimes you need skirts and sometimes you need legs. It's all about balance and harmony and making a pleasing composition that works in practical and aesthetic terms.

FABRICS ARE CLEARLY A MAJOR COMPONENT of comfort because they're what we all touch every day. In most rooms, we like to mix textures so that there's something soft, something sleek, something with a distinctive weave, and maybe just a little bit of leather. As with everything else comfort-related, function factors into how we make our fabric selections.

~~ *In the master bedroom, a French Louis XIV walnut bureau with fantastic ormolu mounts adds depth and patina. The painted four-poster bed with its bed hangings (opposite) is perfectly proportioned for the room, with its high, beautifully detailed ceiling.*

The guesthouse is a charming getaway and, when guests desire, a private retreat. Its high ceilings, elegant detailing, inviting loggia, outdoor bed, and blue-and-white bedroom echo elements of the main house.

The guesthouse takes its light-blue-and-white color palette from the ocean just a few steps away. The room is set up for comfort and practicality, with two full-size four-poster beds resting under the airy cypress ceiling, lounge seating, benches at the foot of the beds, and a writing desk. Sheers at the windows filter the bright daylight and provide privacy.

So much of design is in the details. We pay a lot of attention to the small things, and we prefer subtle, careful embellishments that may not be apparent at first glance.

DETAILS, DETAILS, DETAILS

EVERYONE HAS HIS OR HER OWN OPINION about the decorative details and custom elements that enhance a room. We certainly do. We pay a lot of attention to the little things, because we believe that the care we take with those little things translates into a room that is inviting and welcoming, and really pretty too. As much as we love having the opportunity to create something special and unique, if it involves an element of a room that someone will be living with for a while—for instance, curtains or a sofa—we take an understated approach to embellishment. Our style would be to add a hand-stitched scallop on a hem in matching thread or a lovely shell detail as a curtain trim.

CURTAINS ARE ONE PLACE WHERE DESIGNERS, us included, love to express themselves. We usually frame the windows of our projects in panels of solid, quiet-colored fabrics. We like simple treatments, but they're never quite as simple as they first appear. We always think carefully about the lead edge, the hem, and what sort of pleating we use at the top. Careful details and quiet embellishments can transform that simple curtain into something much more special.

BECAUSE WE WANT THE WINDOWS to look inviting, not distracting, from the street, we line our curtains in a beautiful colored fabric that suits the location. In Charlotte, for instance, we usually use a neutral, putty-colored lining, which looks elegant from the street. In Florida, we might use a pale, pale aqua, sea green, or blue-green—a tone that speaks to the exterior environment.

WE ALWAYS MAKE SURE THAT OUR CURTAINS are fabricated with a lining and a flannel interlining, because that gives them a great fold and an elegant drape, a heft with wonderful presence; it can also help insulate. Interlining comes in different thicknesses; we use the one appropriate for the particular location.

NAILHEAD TRIM ON UPHOLSTERY is a favorite detailing device. It offers endless variety in pattern and makes for a terrific geometric motif, egg and dart, a swirl, and so on. The touch of hardware adds just a little reflectivity into a room. And particularly with leather and suede, nailhead trim is just a natural.

BEAUTIFUL LINENS AT THE TABLE may be everyday luxuries, but they're necessities too—and also considerate details that tell your guests you think they're special, welcome, and appreciated. There are certainly times when we all use paper, but it's nice to use your linens. If the fabric includes a bit of poly, you won't have to iron them. Ultrasuede napkins, for instance, are easy care: just smooth and fold when you take them out of the dryer. And the texture is a delightful surprise.

In the guesthouse loggia, a stone-top table is inviting and practical under a bronze chandelier (opposite). An outdoor bed for reading and lounging is built into the far end of the space. The sofa and lounge chairs have Moroccan-style fretwork details.

For a casual lunch or cocktails alfresco on the loggia overlooking the ocean just steps away, a table set in many shades of blue and aqua seems a natural, delightful fit.

The loggia off the living room looks straight out to the Atlantic Ocean. The area is large enough for a dining table that seats up to ten plus a conversation area with lounge chairs, a sofa, a chaise, and coffee and side tables.

RESOURCES

ANTIQUES
- A. Tyner Antiques, www.swedishantiques.biz
- Christopher Jones Antiques, www.christopherjonesantiques.co.uk
- Circa Interiors and Antiques, www.circaonline.net
- Guinevere Antiques, Ltd., www.guinevere.co.uk
- Jaqueline Adams Antiques, www.jadamsantiques.com
- Jean Francois Nuvielle and Gilles Barges, barse.antiques@gmail.com
- John Rosselli Antiques, www.johnroselliantiques.com
- Marielle and Robin Smither, mariellesmither@me.com
- Parc Monceau Fine Antiques, www.parcmonceauatl.com
- Paris Flea Market, Marche Aux Puces, www.les-puces.com
- Spencer Swaffer Antiques, www.spencerswaffer.co.uk
- The English Room, www.theenglishroom.biz
- The Gables Antiques, www.thegablesantiques.com
- Tom Hayes and Associates and Toby West Limited, tobypwest@gmail.com
- William Word Fine Antiques, www.williamwordantiques.com

ARCHITECTS
- Don Duffy Architecture, www.donduffyarchitecture.com
- JLF and Associates, Inc., www.jlfarchitects.com
- McAlpine Tankersley Architecture, www.mcalpinetankersley.com
- Meyer Greeson Paullin Benson, www.mgpb.com
- Ruard Veltman Architecture Incorporated, www.ruardveltmanarchitecture.com
- Thomas M. Kirchhoff, Architect, www.kirchhoffarchitects.com

ART AND ACCESSORIES
- Claudia Heath Fine Art, www.claudiaheathfineart.com
- Elder Gallery, www.elderart.com
- Elizabeth Bruns, Inc., www.elizabethbruns.com
- Fighting Bear Antiques, Terry Winchell, www.fightingbear.com
- Hidell Brooks Gallery, www.hidellbrooks.com
- J.N. Bartfield Galleries, www.bartfield.com
- Mrs. Howard, www.phoebehoward.net
- Renee George Gallery, www.reneegeorgegallery.com
- Tayloe Piggott Gallery, www.tayloepiggottgallery.com
- Trailside Galleries, www.trailsidegalleries.com
- Treillage, Ltd., www.treillageonline.com
- William Yeoward, www.williamyeowardcrystal.com

BUILDERS
- David R. Webb Builders, Inc., www.webbbuilders.com
- Hubert Whitlock Builders, www.whitlockbuilders.com
- Kaleel Builders, www.kaleelbuilders.com
- On Site Management, Inc., www.onsitemanagement.com
- Paradigm Building Group, LLC, www.paradigmbuildinggroup.com
- Philip R. Thomas Construction Company, www.prtconstruction.com

CUSTOM VENDORS
- AMF Custom Upholstery, amfuph@hotmail.com
- Bourgeoisie, Inc., www.bourgeoisie3d.com
- Burch Company Wood Studio, www.burchcompanywoodstudio.com
- Custom Window Treatments, Inc., www.customwindowtreatmentsinc.com
- Fine Designs, Charlotte, N.C., (704) 544-7733
- Fosters Installations, Brian Foster, draperyguy@yahoo.com
- H&F Upholstering, Inc., Charlotte, N.C., (704) 332-5230
- Michael W. Greene Antique Reproductions and Restorations, www.michaelgreenereproductions.com
- Monarch Woodcrafting, stevemorgan@carolina.rr.com
- Rugworks, Inc., redii2000@aol.com

DESIGN SHOWROOMS
- Ainsworth-Noah, www.ainsworth-noah.com
- Donghia, www.donghia.com
- Ernest Gaspard and Associates, www.ernestgaspard.com
- Grizzel and Mann, Inc., www.grizzelandmann.com
- Holly Hunt, www.hollyhunt.com
- J. Nelson and Company, www.jnelson.com
- Jerry Pair and Associates, Inc., www.jerrypair.com
- John Rosselli Antiques, www.johnroselliantiques.com
- Kravet, Inc., www.kravet.com
- Rogers and Goffigon, Ltd., www.delanyandlong.com/whoweare.cfm
- Travis and Company, www.travisandcompany.com

FLORAL DESIGNERS
- Flower Hardware, Cecelia Heffernan, www.flowerhardware.com
- In Bloom, Ltd., Jay Lugibihl, www.inbloomltd.com

FRAMING
- Art Aspects, www.artaspects.biz
- Avery Art, Evelyn Avery, www.averyart.com
- Gunn's Quality Glass and Mirror, Inc., www.gunnsqualityglass.com
- Fred Reed Picture Framing, Inc., www.fredreedinc.com

FURNITURE
- Baker Furniture, www.bakerfurniture.com
- Beeline Home by Bunny Williams, www.bunnywilliams.com/beeline/
- Brown Jordan, www.brownjordan.com
- Cameron Collection, www.cameroncollection.com
- Central Station Original Interiors, Inc., www.centralstationinteriors.com
- Chelsea Textiles, www.chelseatextiles.com/us/
- Darnell and Company, www.darnellandcompany.com
- Dennis and Leen, www.dennisandleen.com
- Formations, www.formationsusa.com
- Homefires, www.homefiresusa.com
- Janus et Cie, www.janusetcie.com
- Kingsley-Bate, www.kingsleybate.com
- Lee Industries, www.leeindustries.com
- McKinnon and Harris, www.mckinnonharris.com
- Munder Skiles, LLC, www.munder-skiles.com
- Niermann Weeks, www.niermannweeks.com
- Restoration Hardware, www.restorationhardware.com
- Rose Tarlow Melrose House, www.rosetarlow.com
- The Hickory Chair Furniture Co., www.hickorychair.com
- Verellen, Inc., www.verellen.biz

LANDSCAPE ARCHITECTS
- Bruce Clodfelter and Associates, www.bruceclodfelter.com
- Nievera Williams Designs, Mario Nievera, www.nieverawilliams.com
- Page Duke Landscape Architects, Ben Page, www.pageduke.com
- Verdone Landscape Architects, Jim Verdone, www.verdonelandarch.com

LIGHTING
- Dennis and Leen, www.dennisandleen.com
- Edgar-Reeves Lighting and Antiques, www.edgar-reeves.com
- Evan Wood Chandelier and Lighting, evan.h.wood@gmail.com
- Formations, www.formationsusa.com
- Lucy Cope, Ltd., www.lucycope.com
- Lux Fine Lampshades, www.luxlampshades.com
- McLean Lighting Works, www.mcleanlighting.com
- Paul Ferrante, Inc., www.paulferrante.com
- Phillips and Wood, John Phillips, www.phillipsandwood.co.uk
- The Urban Electric Company, www.urbanelectricco.com
- Vaughan Designs, www.vaughandesigns.com
- Visual Comfort and Co., www.visualcomfort.com

LINENS
- Chelsea Textiles, Ltd., www.chelseatextiles.com/us/
- Home Treasures Fine Linens and Textiles, www.hometreasureslinens.com
- Julia B., www.juliab.com
- Leontine Linens, www.leontinelinens.com
- Libeco Home, www.libeco.com
- Matouk, www.matouk.com
- Matteo, www.matteohome.com
- Peacock Alley, www.peacockalley.com
- Pine Cone Hill, www.pineconehill.com
- Sferra Fine Linens, www.sferra.com
- Bagni Volpi Noemi, Inc, N.C. Souther Fine Linens, www.bvn-inc.com

RUGS
- ALT for Living, www.altforliving.com
- Barrier Island, www.barrierislandrugs.com
- Charlotte Rug Gallery, www.charlotteruggallery.com
- Designer Carpets, Inc., www.designer-carpets.net
- Eliko Antique and Decorative Rugs, www.elikorugs.com
- Elizabeth Eakins, Inc., www.elizabetheakins.com
- Eve, Inc., www.eveoxfordrugs.com
- Keivan Woven Arts, www.keivanwovenarts.com
- Merida Meridian, www.meridameridian.com
- Stark Carpet, www.starkcarpet.com

SPECIALTY PAINTERS/ARTISTS
- Fe Fi Faux, Greensboro, N.C., (336) 272-3289
- Rick Newton and Jessica O'Nell, Deerfield Beach, Fla., (561) 714-8442
- Terry Reitzel, Charlotte, N.C., (704) 376-9600
- Tony Montognese, www.tonymontognesefinishing.com

ACKNOWLEDGMENTS

OUR GRATITUDE TO OUR CLIENTS—our friends—is beyond expression. We are deeply honored to have had a hand in creating your homes. It's a designer's greatest privilege to contribute to the rooms where you share the best of yourselves with your family and friends and where life's moments become treasured memories. Thank you all for allowing us the opportunity to do just that!

Without Beverly Edens, our gifted friend, we never would have done this book. Beverly, you have our endless gratitude for bringing us the idea, doing the research that enabled us to begin the process, and introducing us to Jill Cohen and Doug Turshen, the very best in the industry!

Our deepest appreciation goes to our marvelous agent Jill Cohen, whose tenacity made our book a reality. Thank you, Jill, for recognizing our potential. We couldn't have done this without your impeccable guidance, your honesty, and your encouragement every step of the way.

Doug Turshen, you are fantastically talented! We cannot thank you enough for your intrinsic gifts, your endless enthusiasm, your keen attention to detail, and especially for these gorgeous graphics, which present our work so very beautifully.

We are endlessly indebted to Kathleen Jayes, our editor at Rizzoli, for giving us this great opportunity. Kathleen, we are so grateful that you recognized our passion for creating comfortable, beautiful homes.

Our most special thanks go to Laura Resen, our principal photographer. We feel privileged to be on the receiving end of her patient demand for excellence, her impeccable eye, her unwavering professional focus, and her tireless effort to get each photograph perfect. Our deep appreciation goes as well to Dylan Chandler, Laura's assistant photographer, who complements Laura in every way.

It has been an absolute pleasure to work with the very talented Judith Nasatir, our brilliant, tireless, and always positive writer. Judith, you have captured our voices and given perfect expression to our thoughts. For that, we are boundlessly thankful.

Jay Lugibihl, our extremely gifted floral designer, abounds in enthusiasm and creative energy. His talents were an integral part of making this book, and we are grateful for his participation.

Lindsay Boner, our dedicated and incredibly organized right hand at Circa, knows how much we appreciate her. We are grateful for her steady and calm nature, tireless efforts on behalf of our clients, attention to detail, and ability to implement the installations of these fabulous houses.

To all of the dear, talented people who make Circa a great family, we thank you for the countless contributions you have made to our projects along the way: Lydia Anders, Cam Davis, Rebecca Davis, Patricia Flachs, Karla Gonzalez, Janelle Hansberger, Whitney Johnson, Patrick Lewis, Arevat Manurachova, Addison Ruffin, Heather Smith, Kathy Smith, Eleanor Stanley, Whitney Sturge, Catherine Walters and Emily Williams.

The endlessly creative Bobby McAlpine is a once-in-a-lifetime friend and colleague. Bobby, we are so grateful for the many design opportunities that your marvelous houses have given us over the years.

There is no one quite like Bunny Williams, our wonderful, creative, generous friend. Bunny has truly inspired and mentored us and countless other designers by so freely sharing her wealth of knowledge through her gorgeous interiors, her books, and her product designs. We admire her amazing style, and we offer our boundless thanks for the beautiful foreword she has written for our book!

To our many close professional friends, advisors, and antiquarians, we have only the greatest admiration and thanks: Gilles Barse and Jean Francois Nuvielle, Christopher Jones, Spencer Swaffer, and Marielle and Robin Smither, it is such a pleasure to work with you. Christine Pearson, our communications guru in Charlotte, thank you for all your bright ideas and advertising savvy.

And finally, for our many clients whose homes are not featured in these pages and for all our wonderful Circa customers, we could not be more appreciative of your patronage, support, and loyalty over the years.

First published in the United States of America in 2013
by Rizzoli International Publications, Inc.
300 Park Avenue South
New York, NY 10010
www.rizzoliusa.com

Photography credits:
Laura Rosen: reverse front endpapers, 2-3, 6, 16, 18-21, 23-31, 34-39,
[Courtesy of Veranda: 51-71], 73-119, 127-187, 207-235

Fritz von der Schulenberg: endpapers, 15, 22, 32, 33, 40-49, 120-125,
reverse back endpapers

Chris Edwards: 189-205

Patricia Lyons: 9

2013 2014 2015 2016 / 10 9 8 7 6 5 4 3 2

Distributed in the U.S. trade by Random House, New York

Printed in China

Design by Doug Turshen with David Huang

ISBN-13: 978-0-8478-3989-6

Library of Congress Catalog Control Number: 2012947377